ADORABLE ELEPHANT DESIGNS

Adult Coloring Book

Stress –Relieving Elephant Designs For Adult

FOR YOUR PATRONAGE

g your feedback and I read every single review

Plea.. ..d your comment, ideas, compliments and anything else to me at:

ebukindle1986@gmail.com

Visit my Author page @: http://www.amazon.com/author/donwilliams

Copyright © 2015, By: DON WILLIAMS

Printed in the United States of American

All Rights Reserved. No part of this publication may be reproduced in any form or by any means, including scanning, photocopying, or otherwise without prior written permission of the copyright holder.

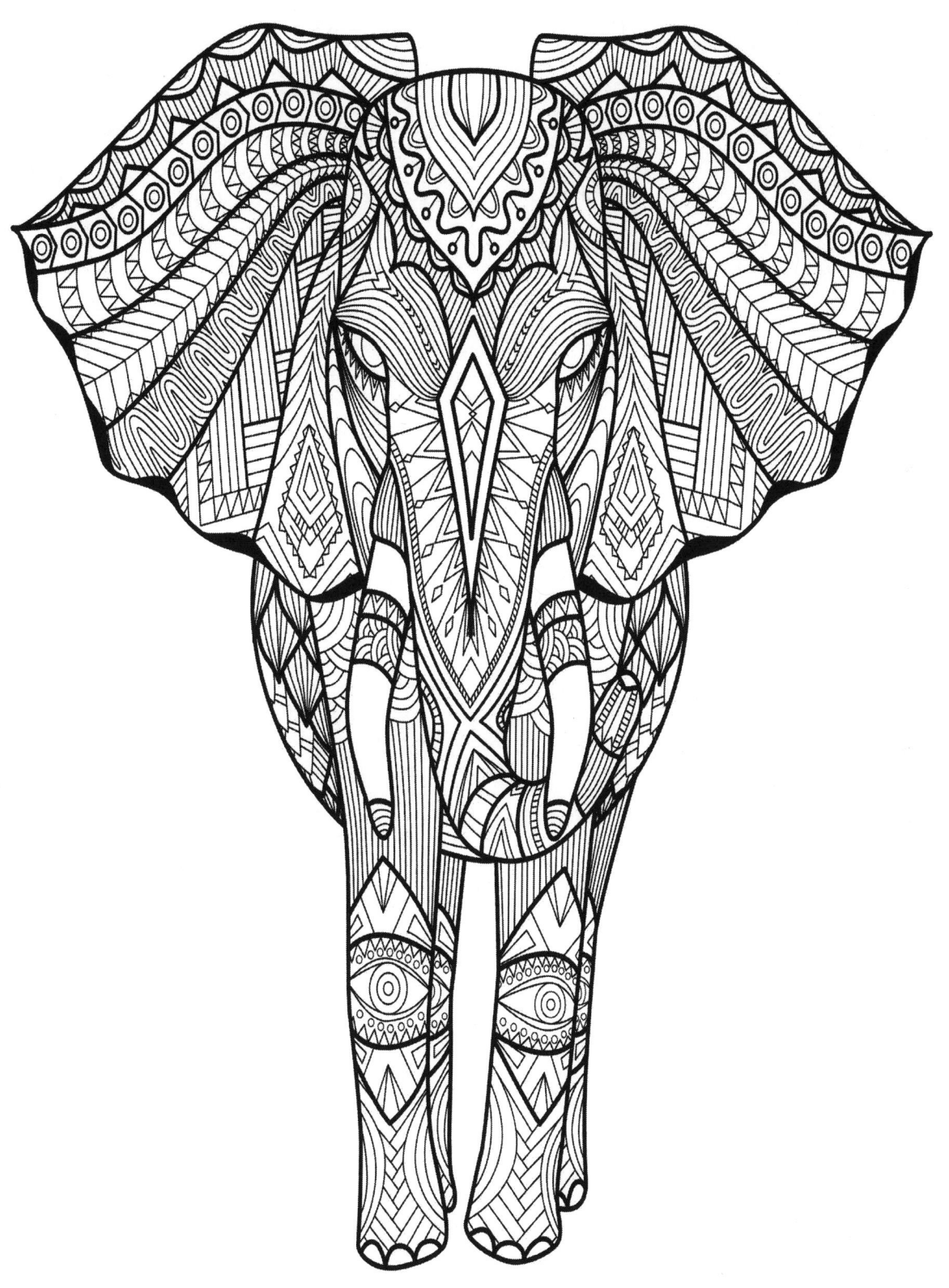

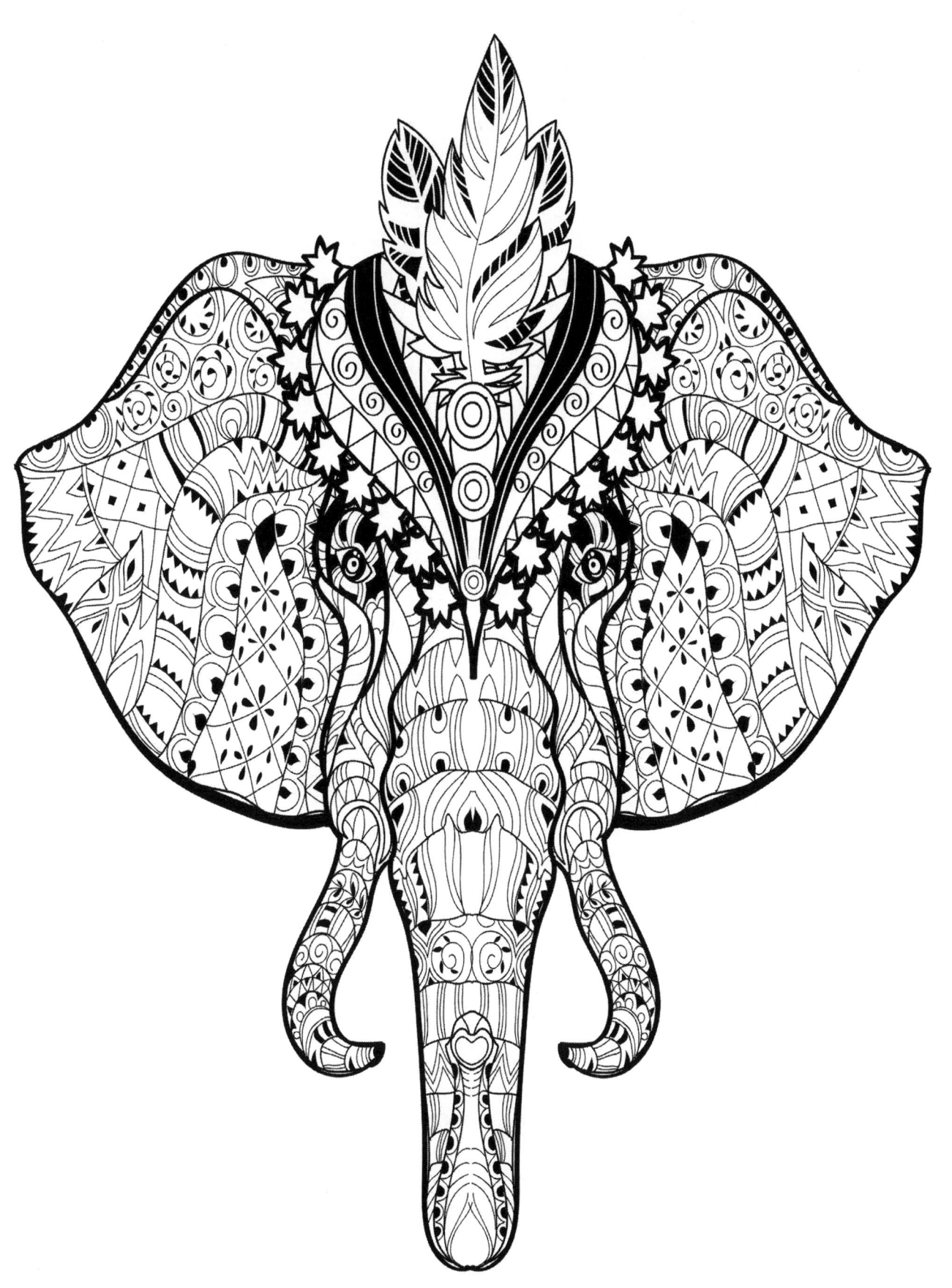

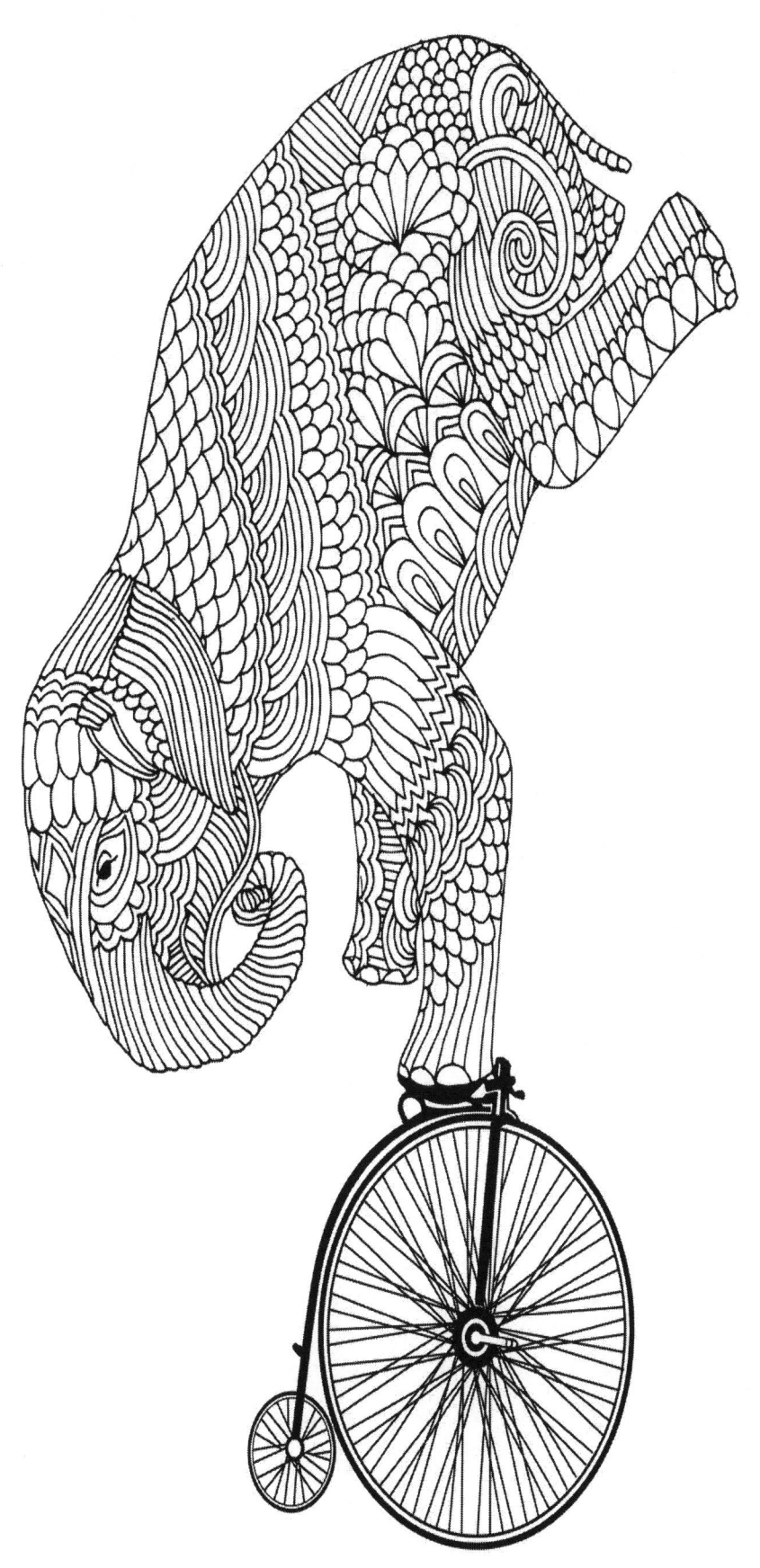

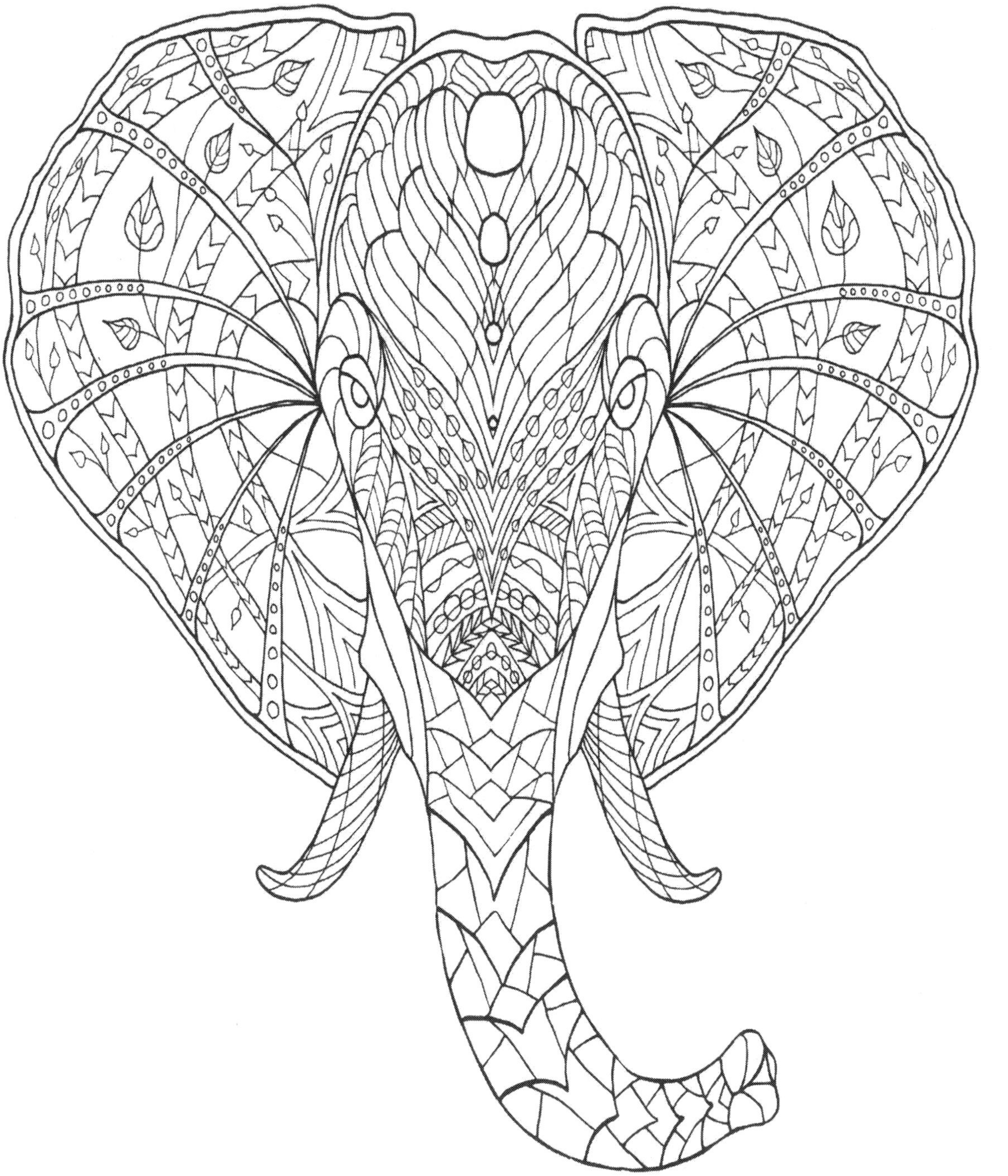

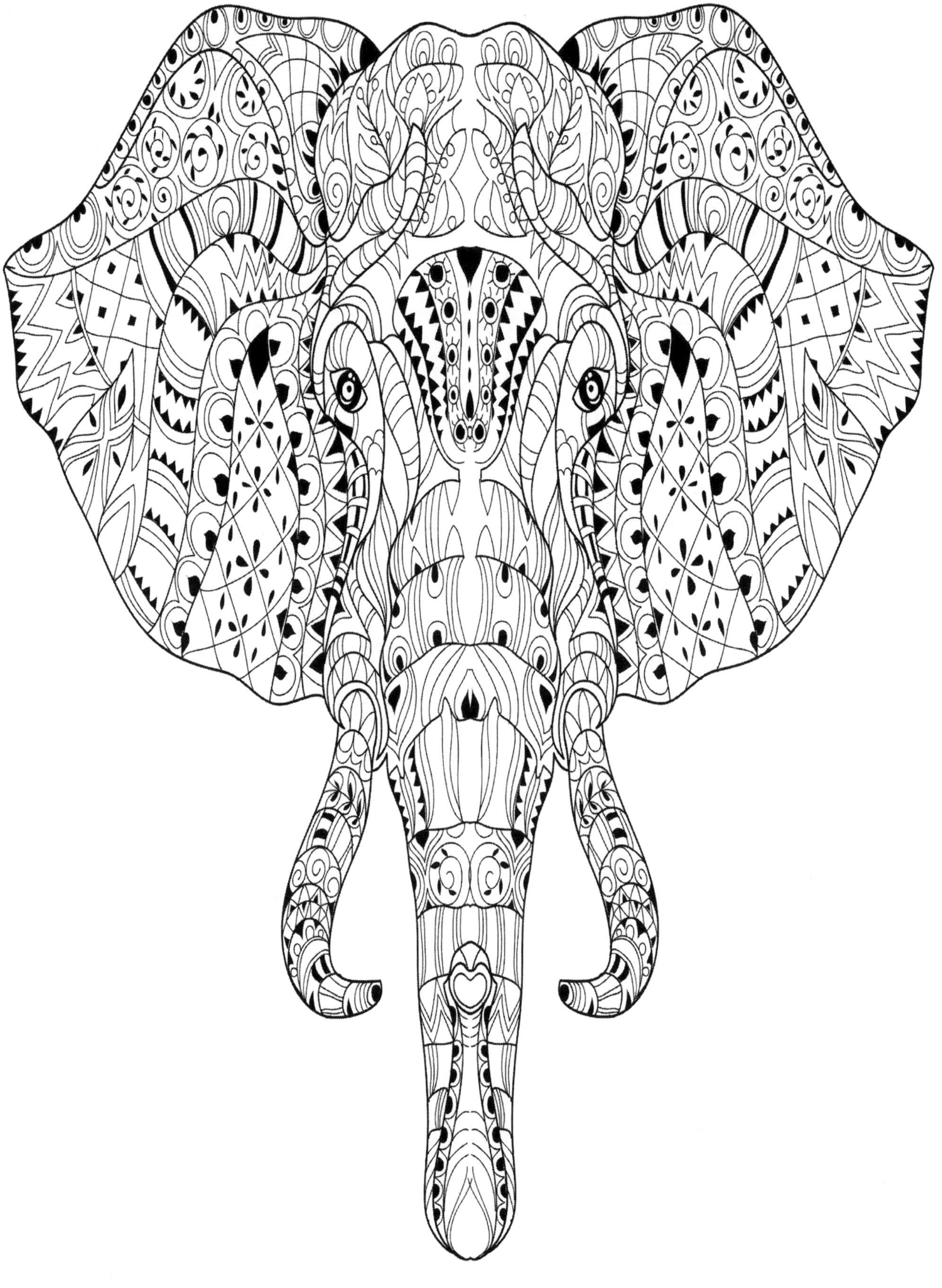

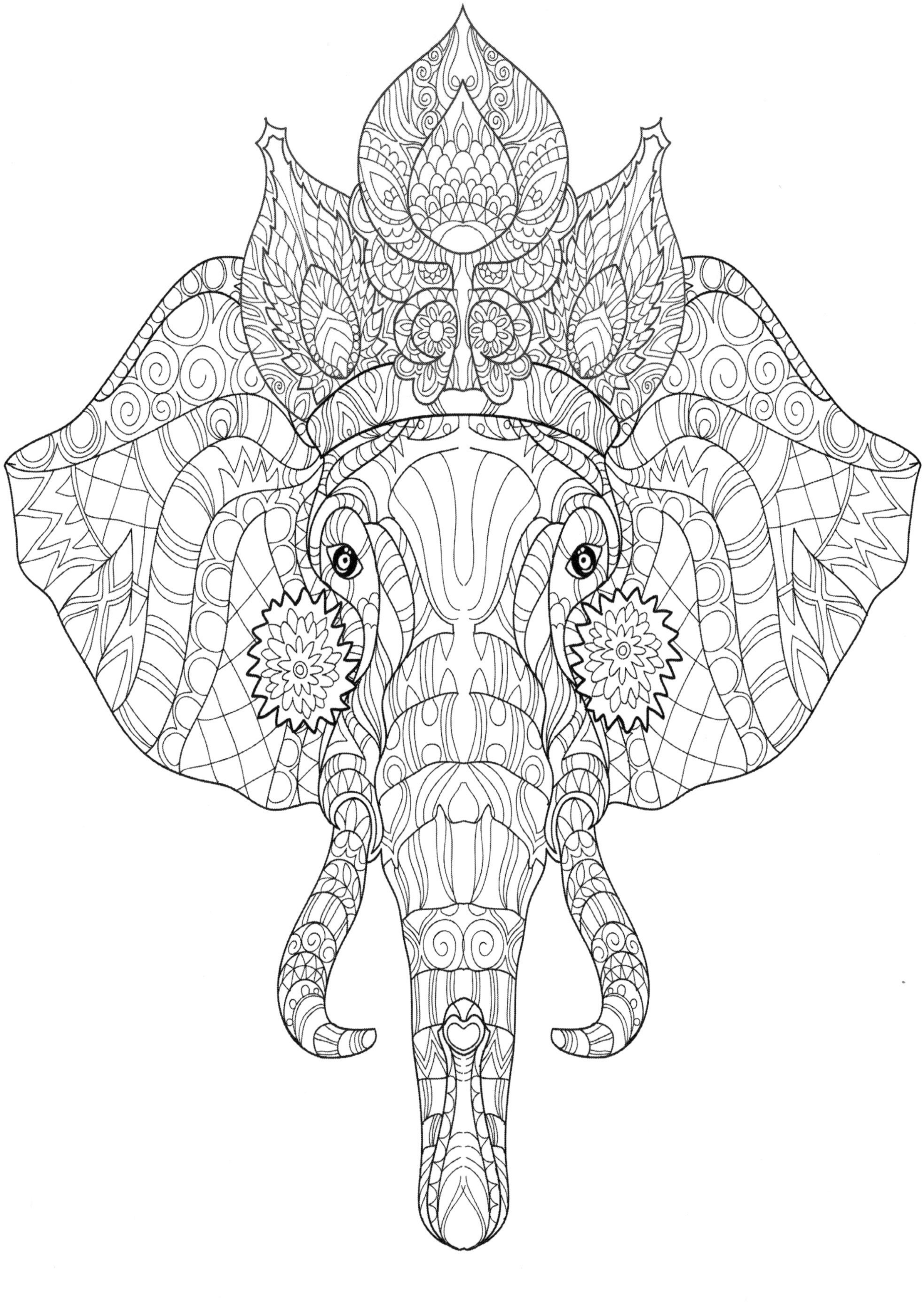

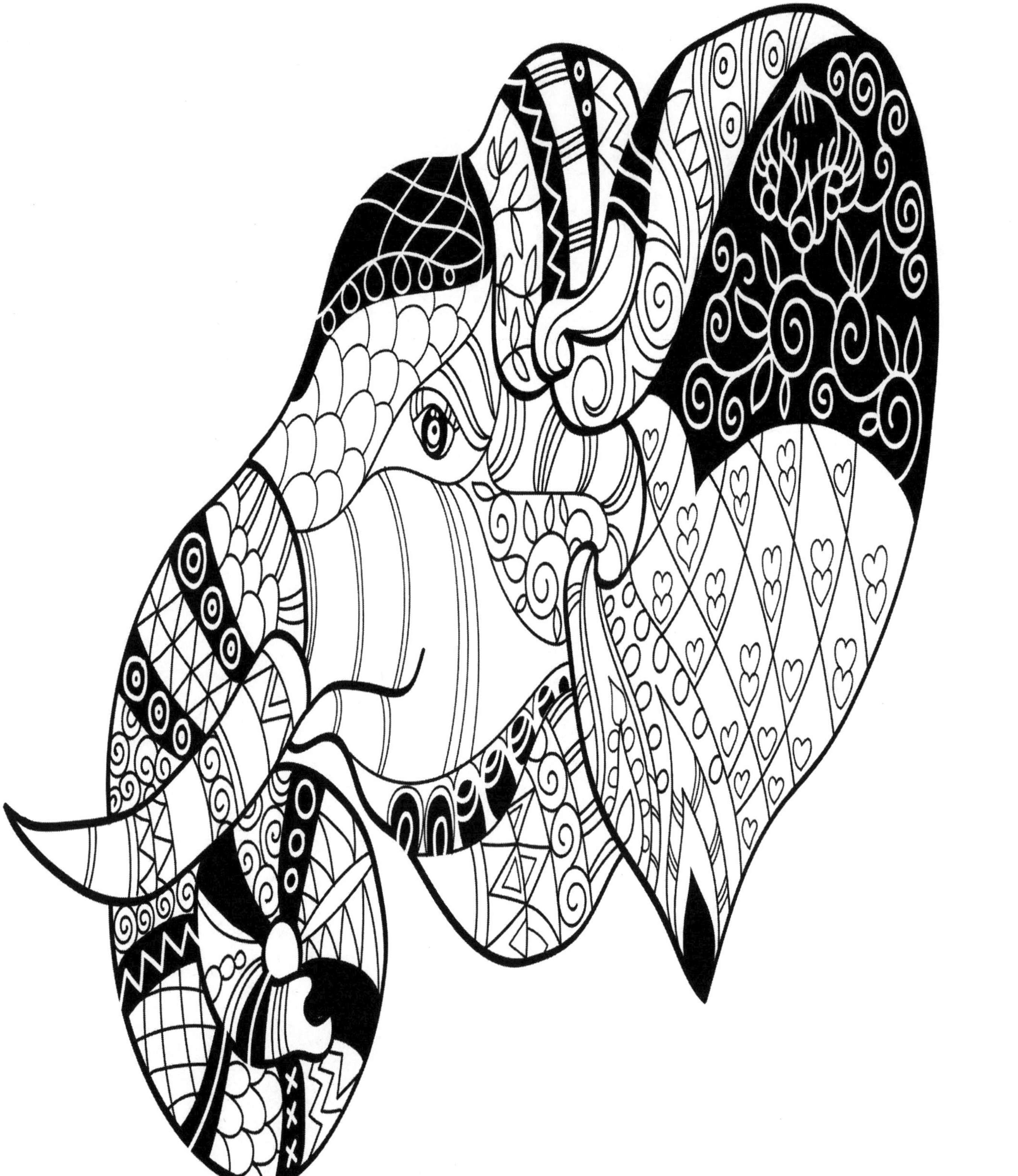

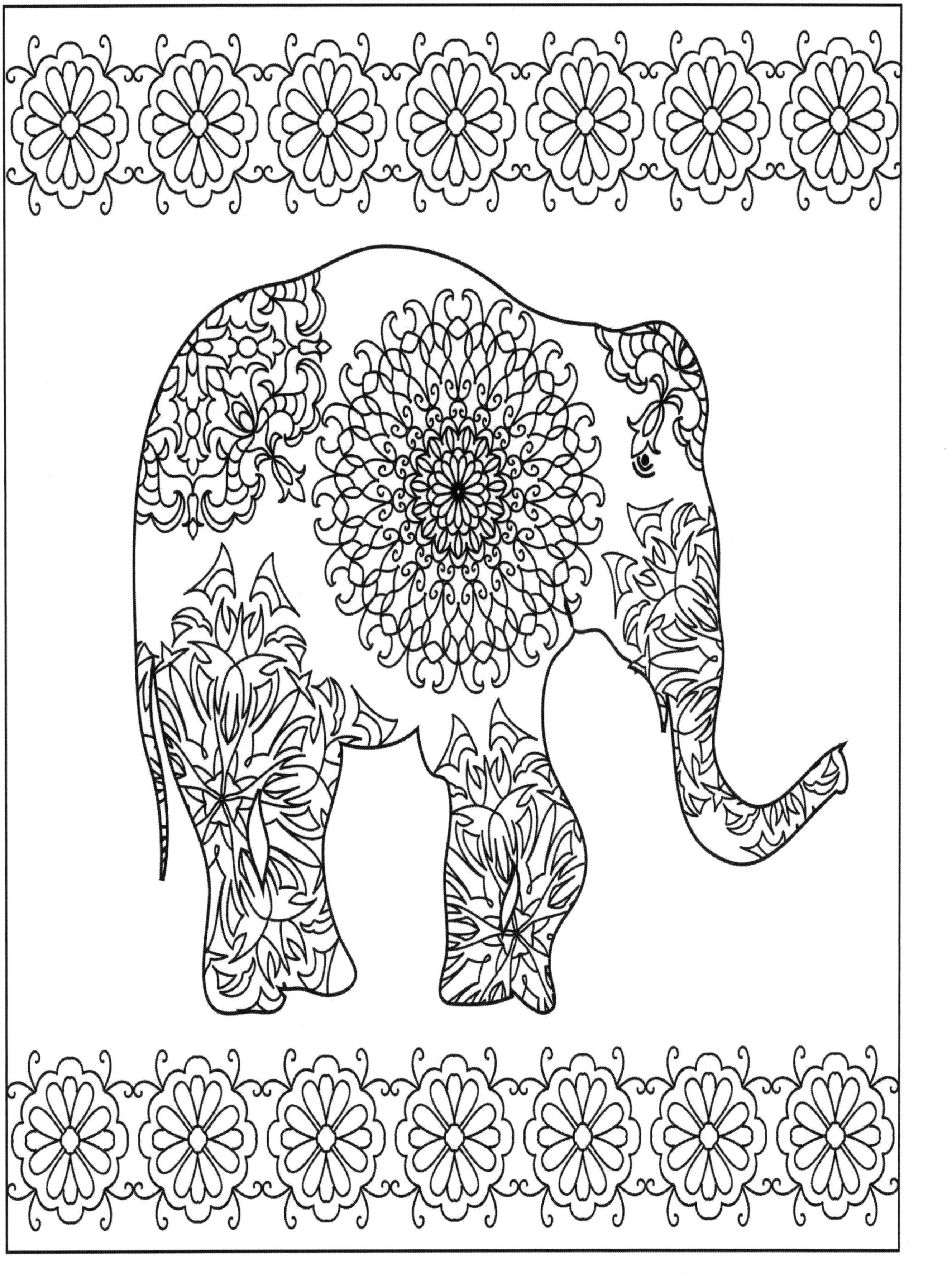

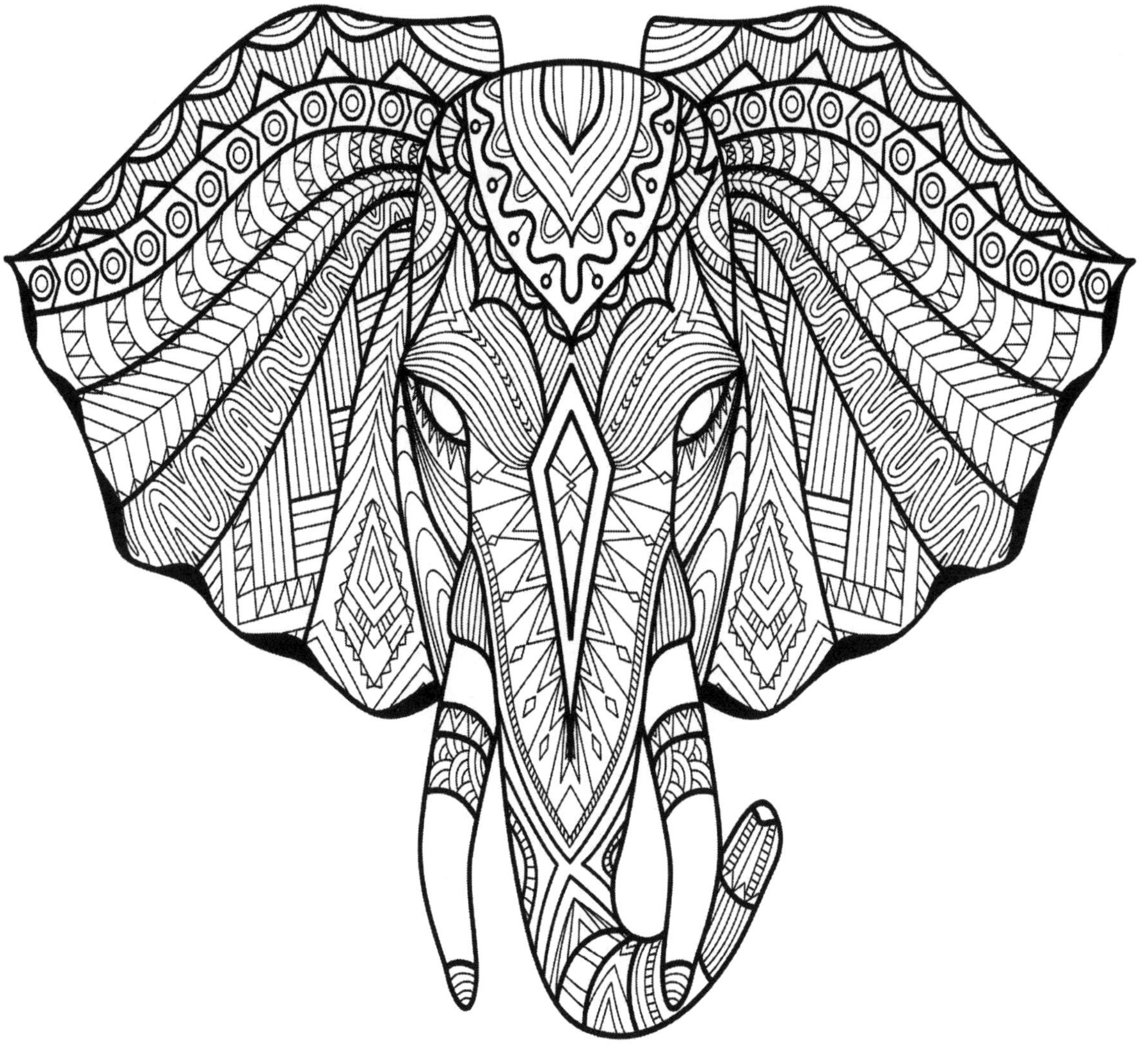

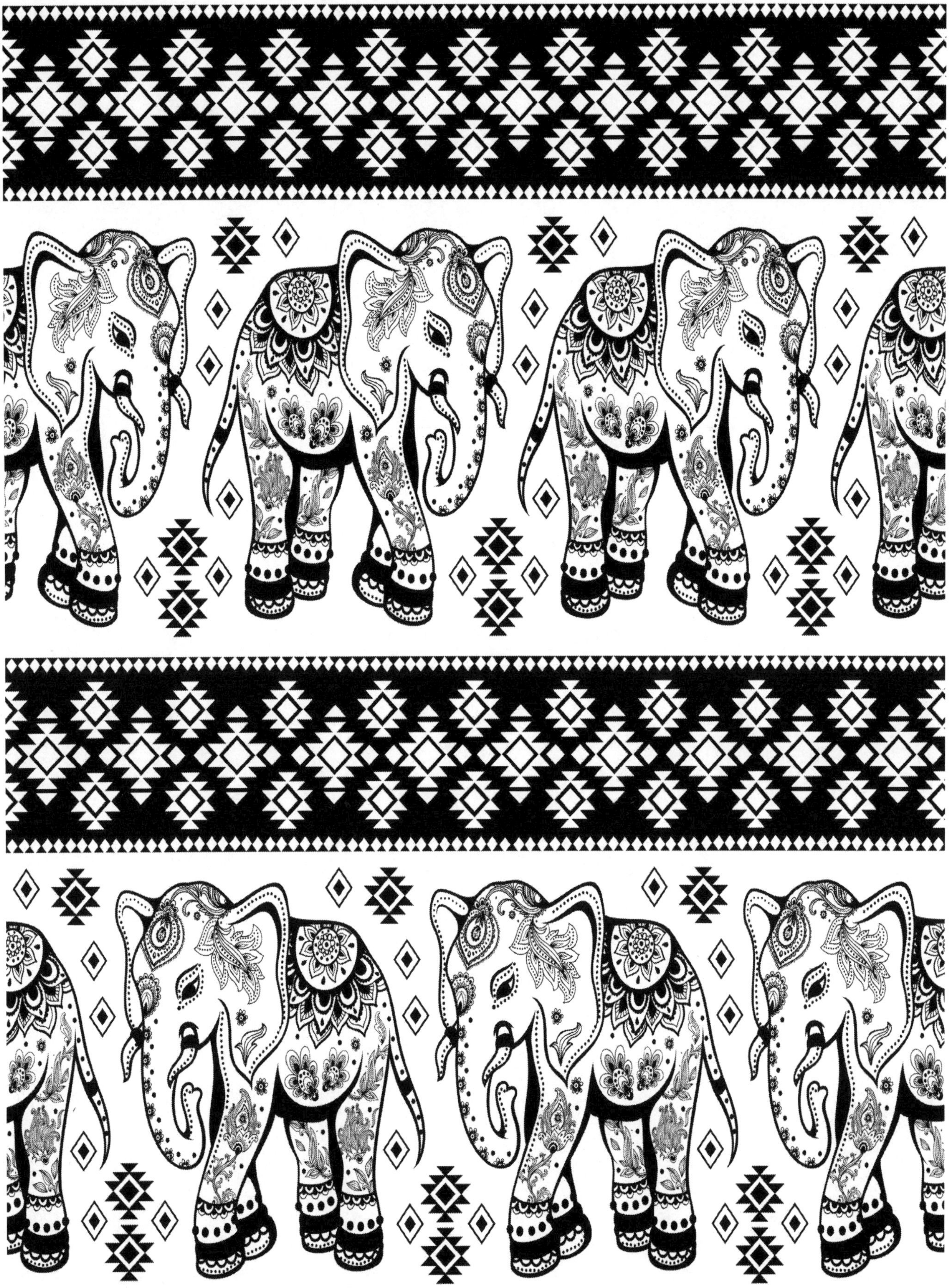

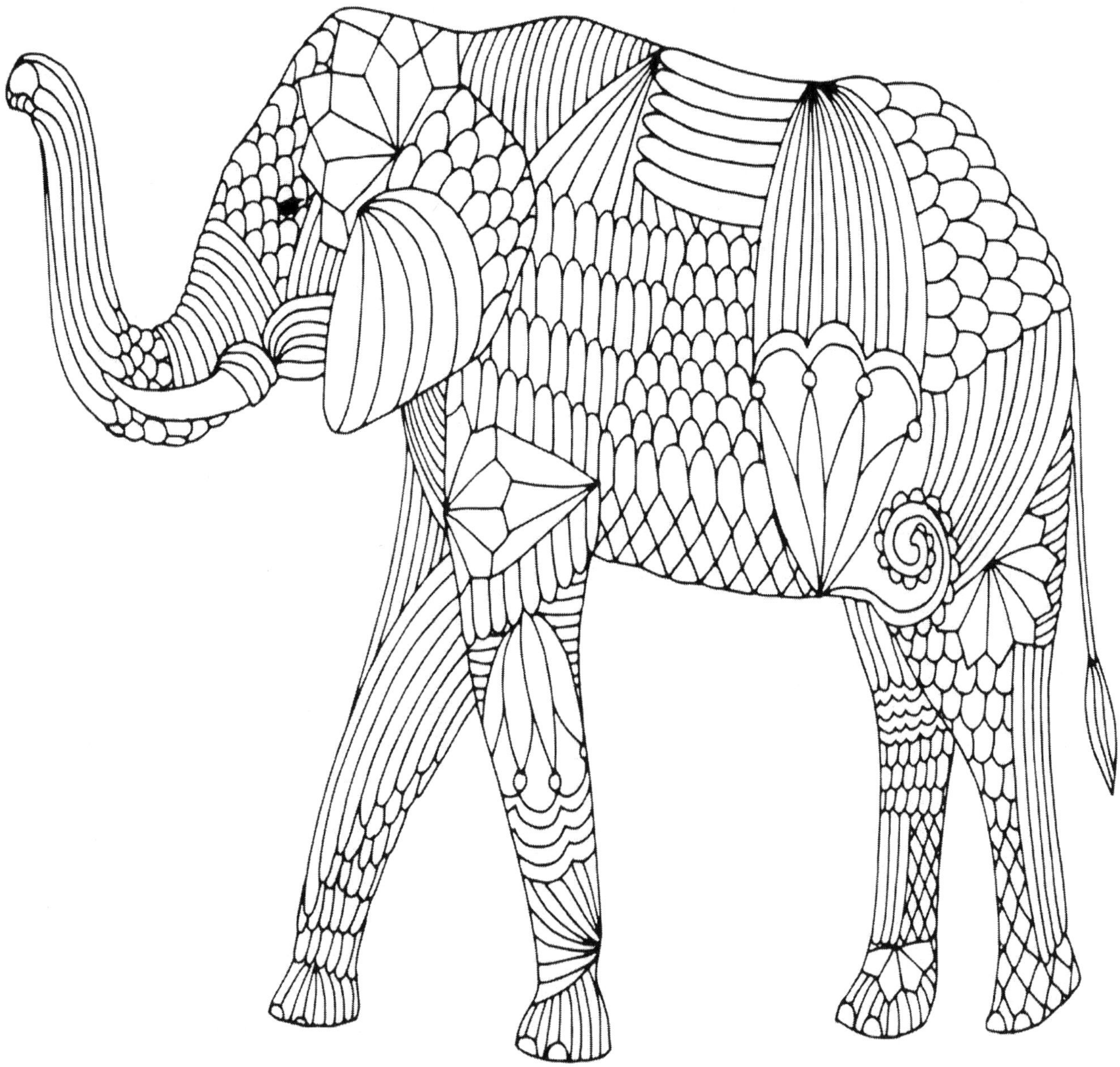

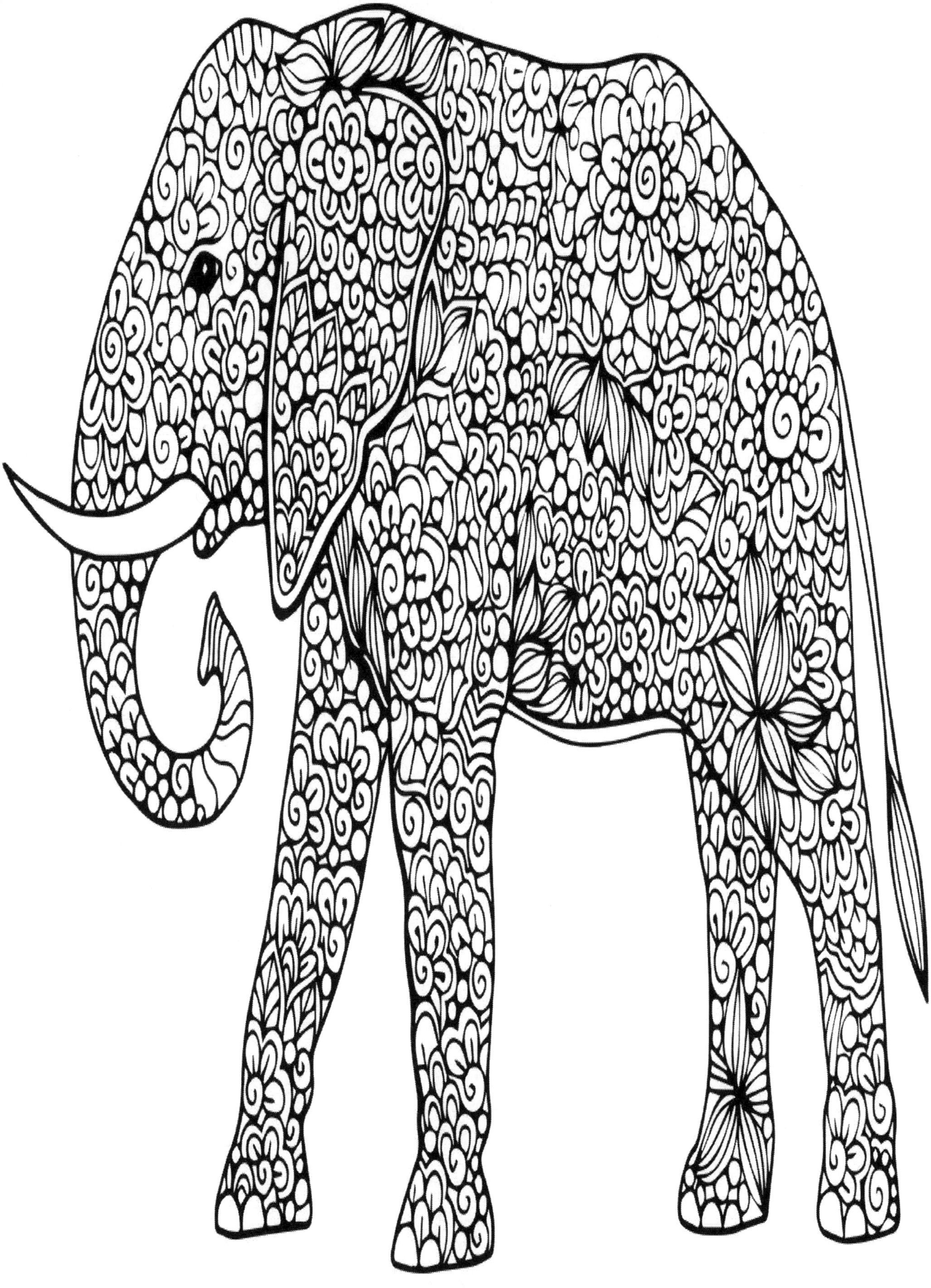

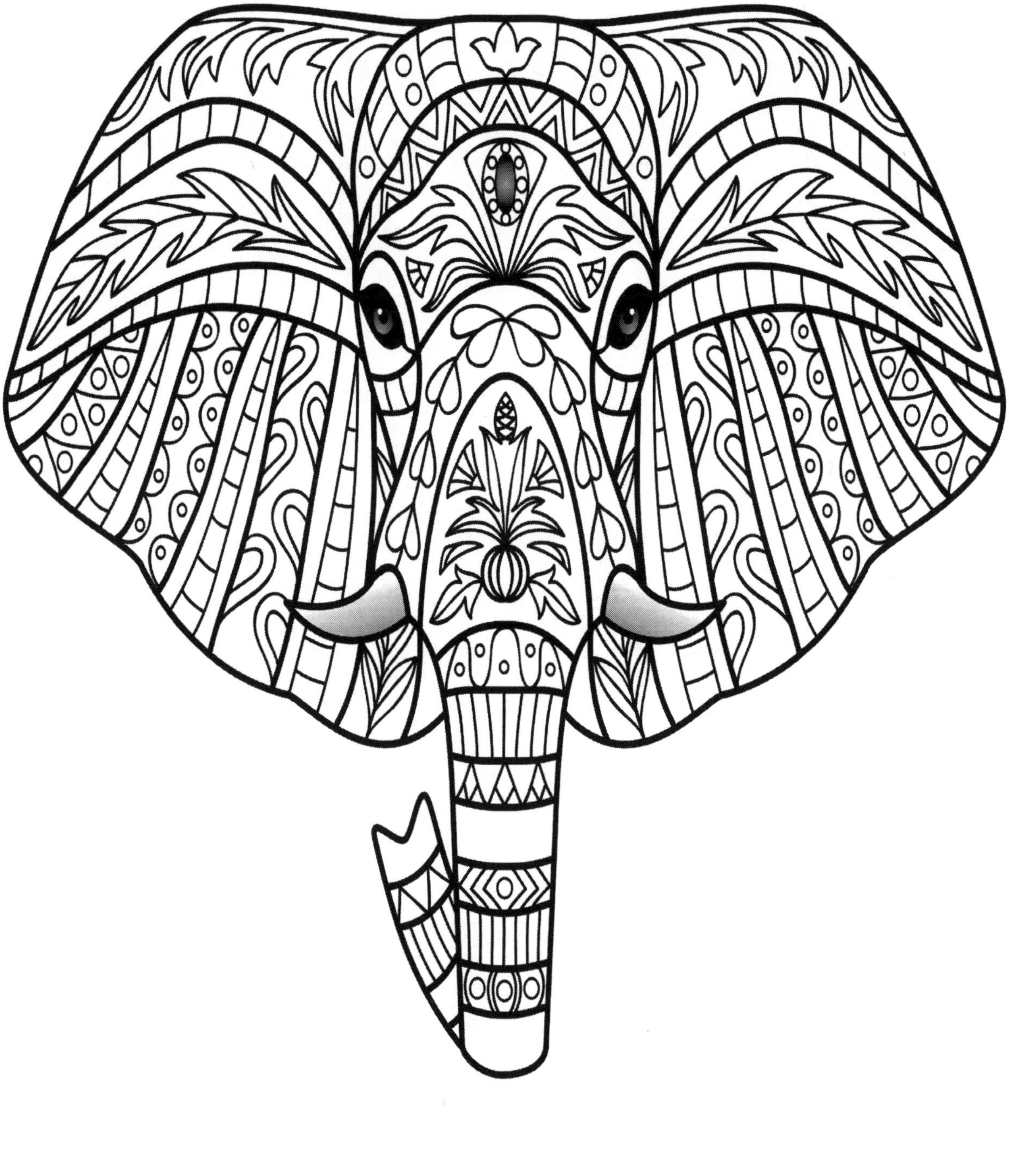

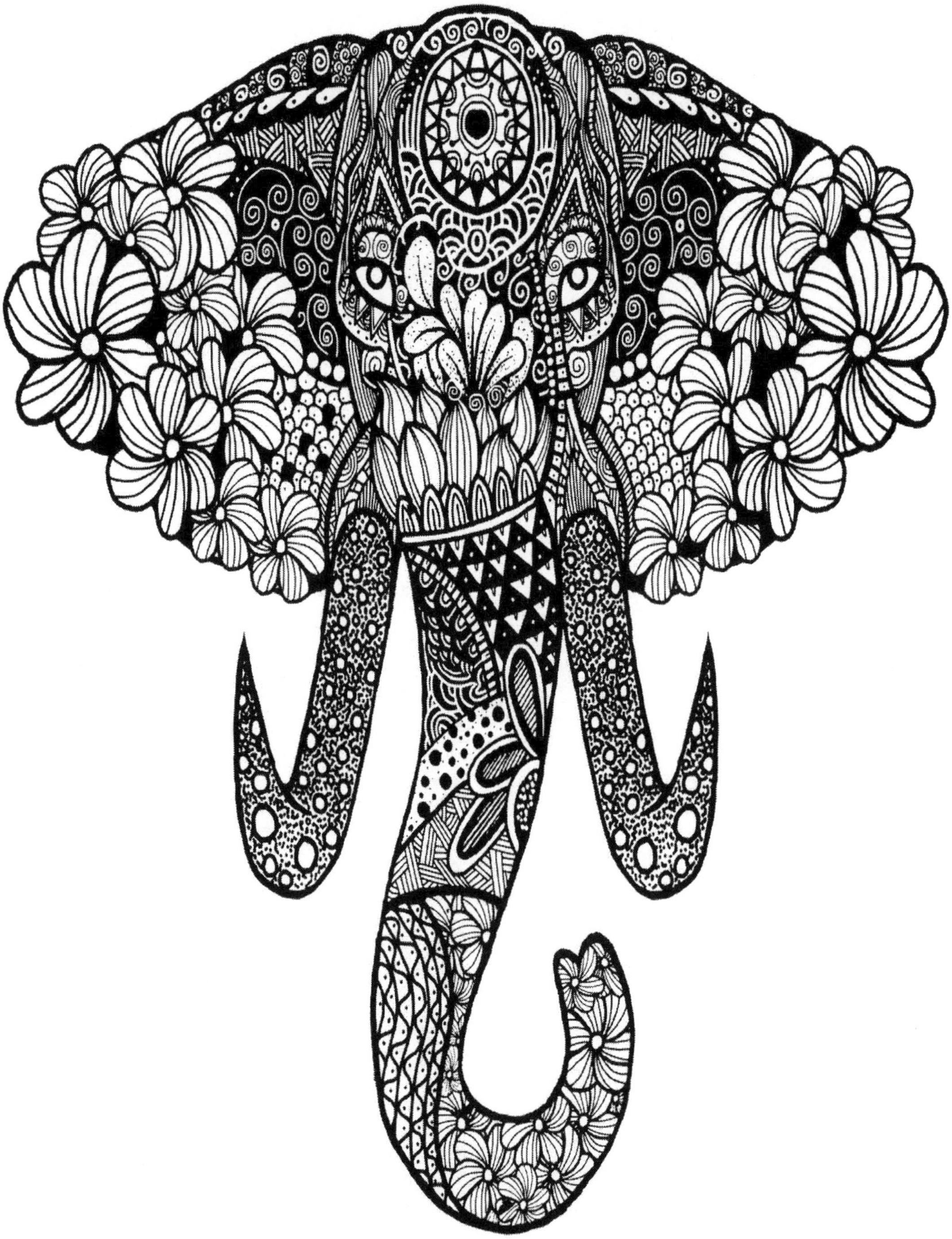

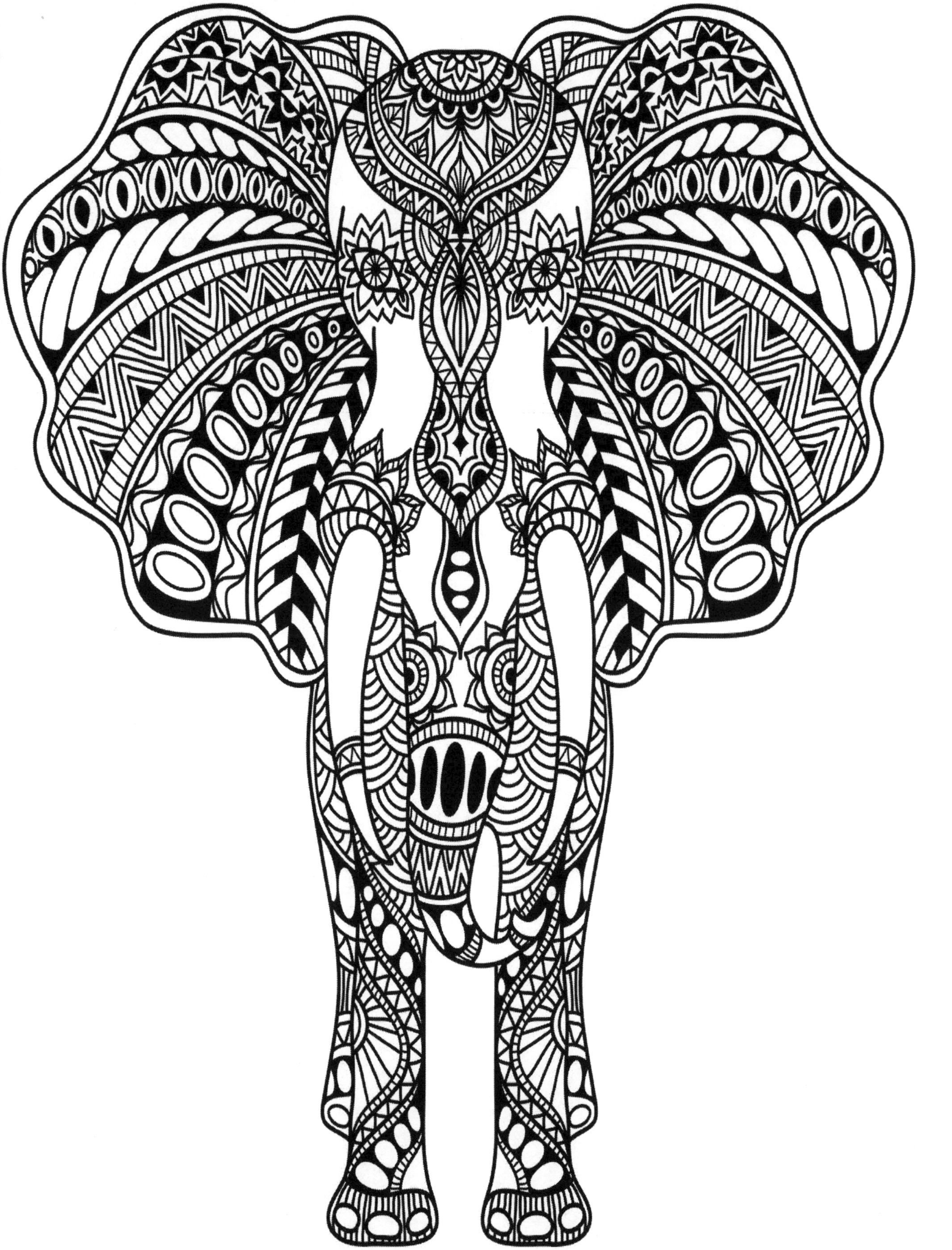

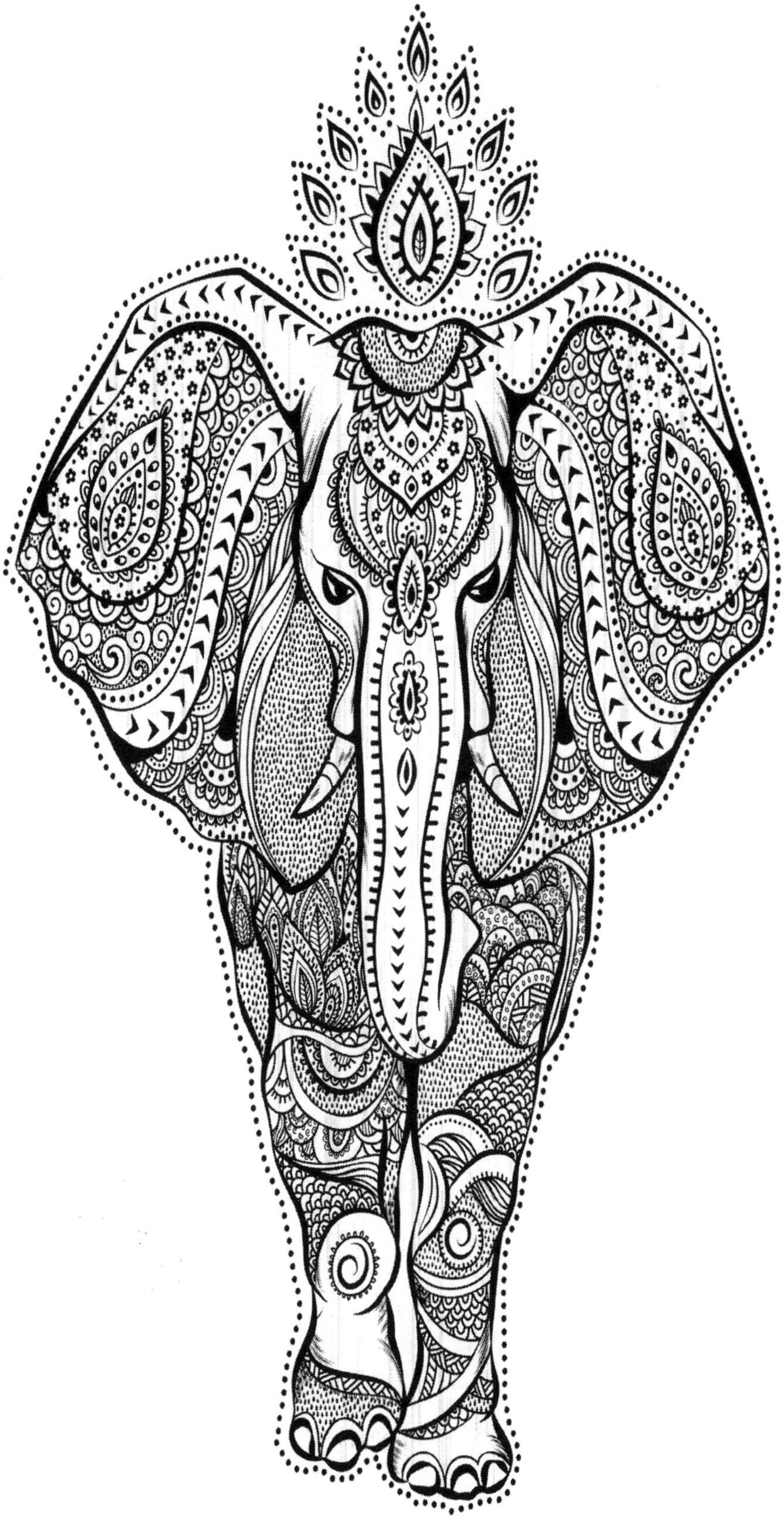

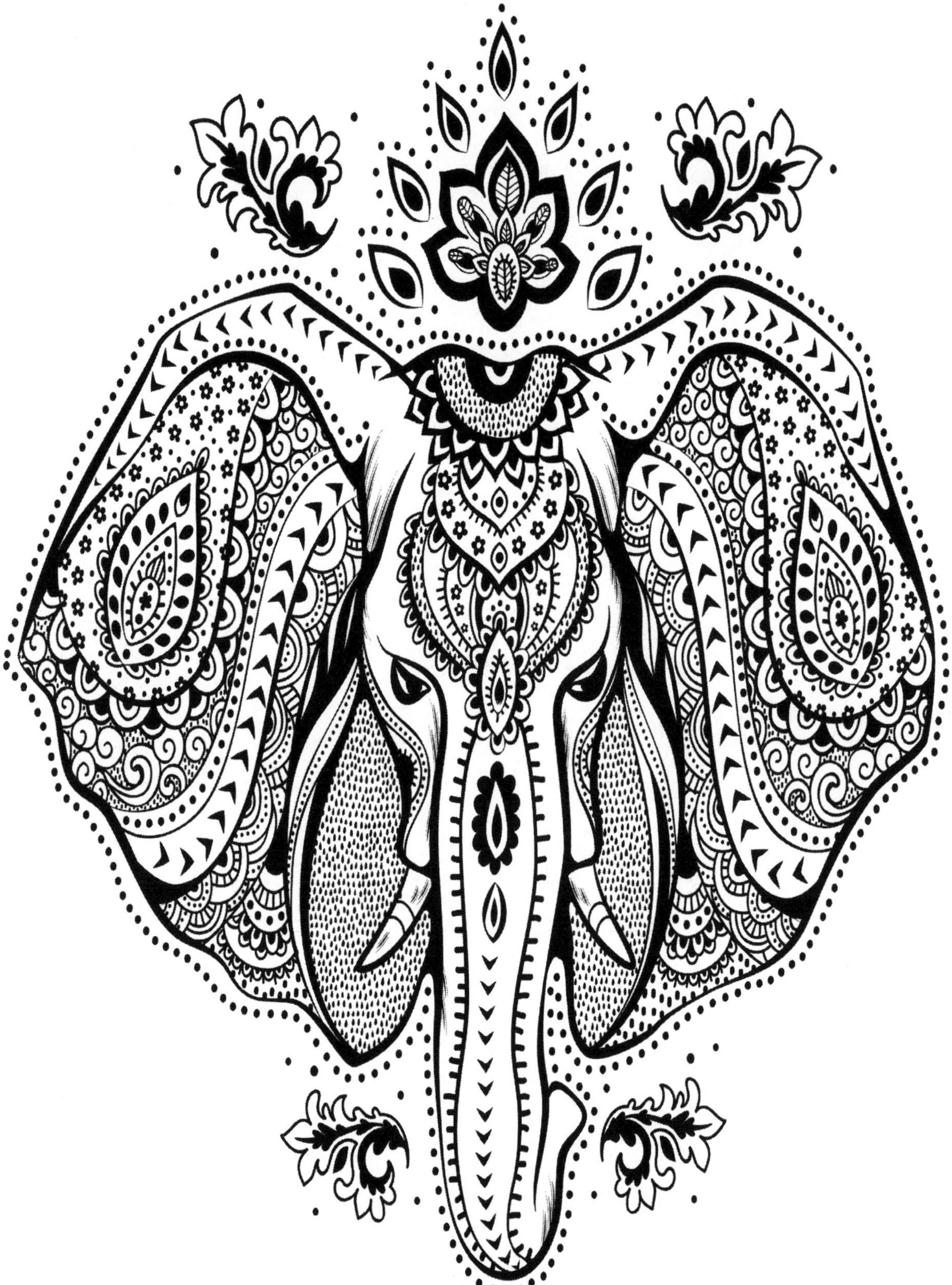

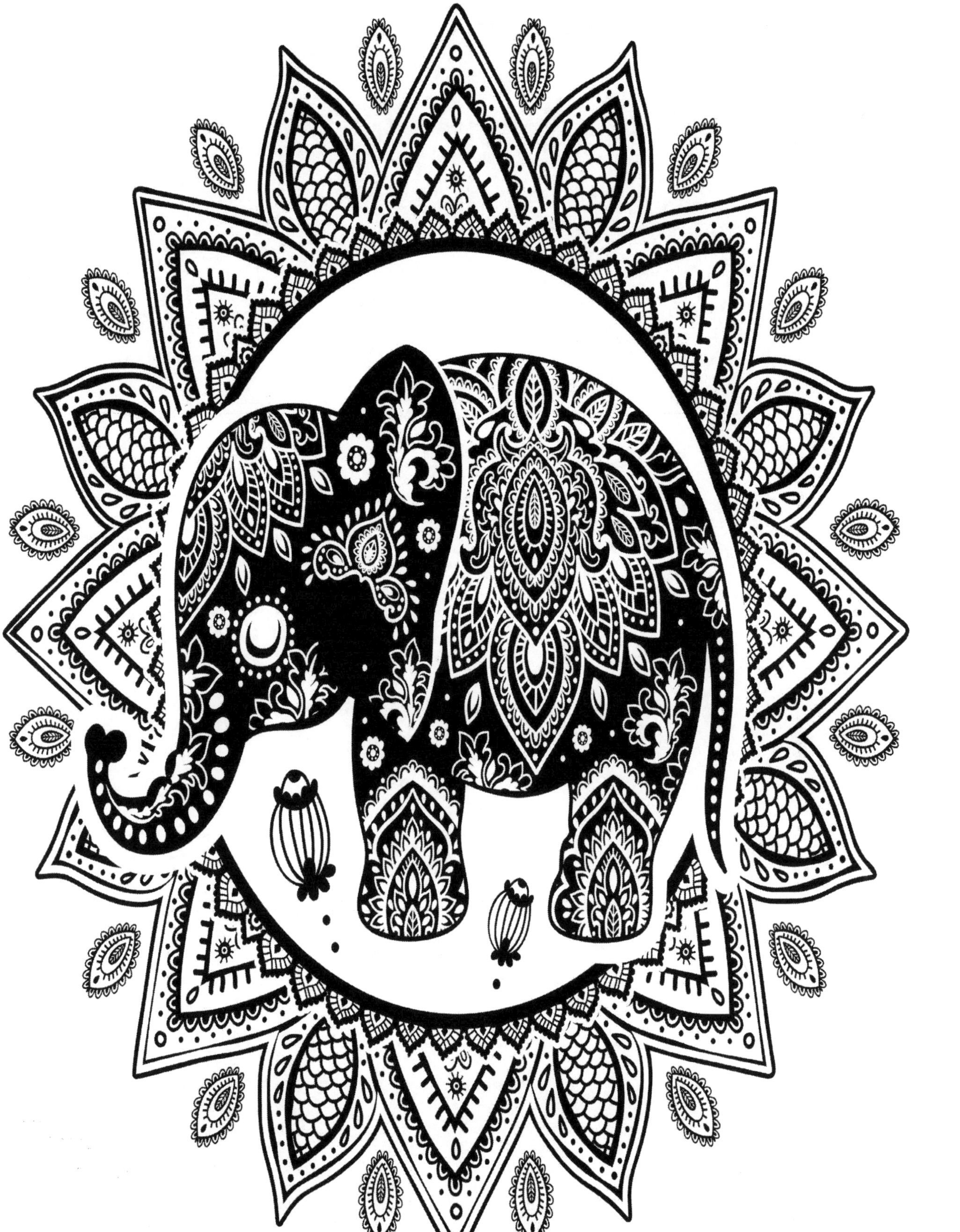

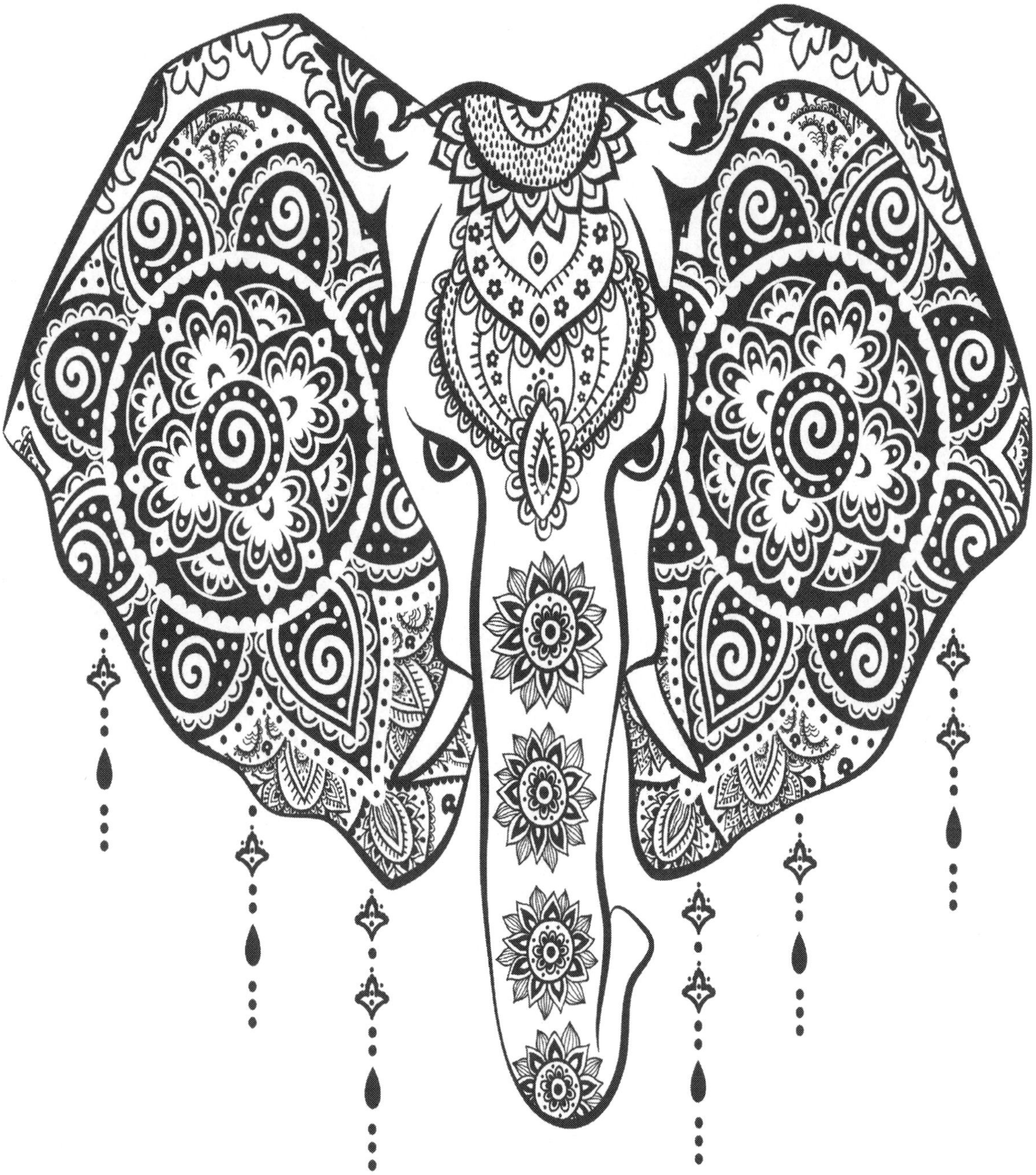

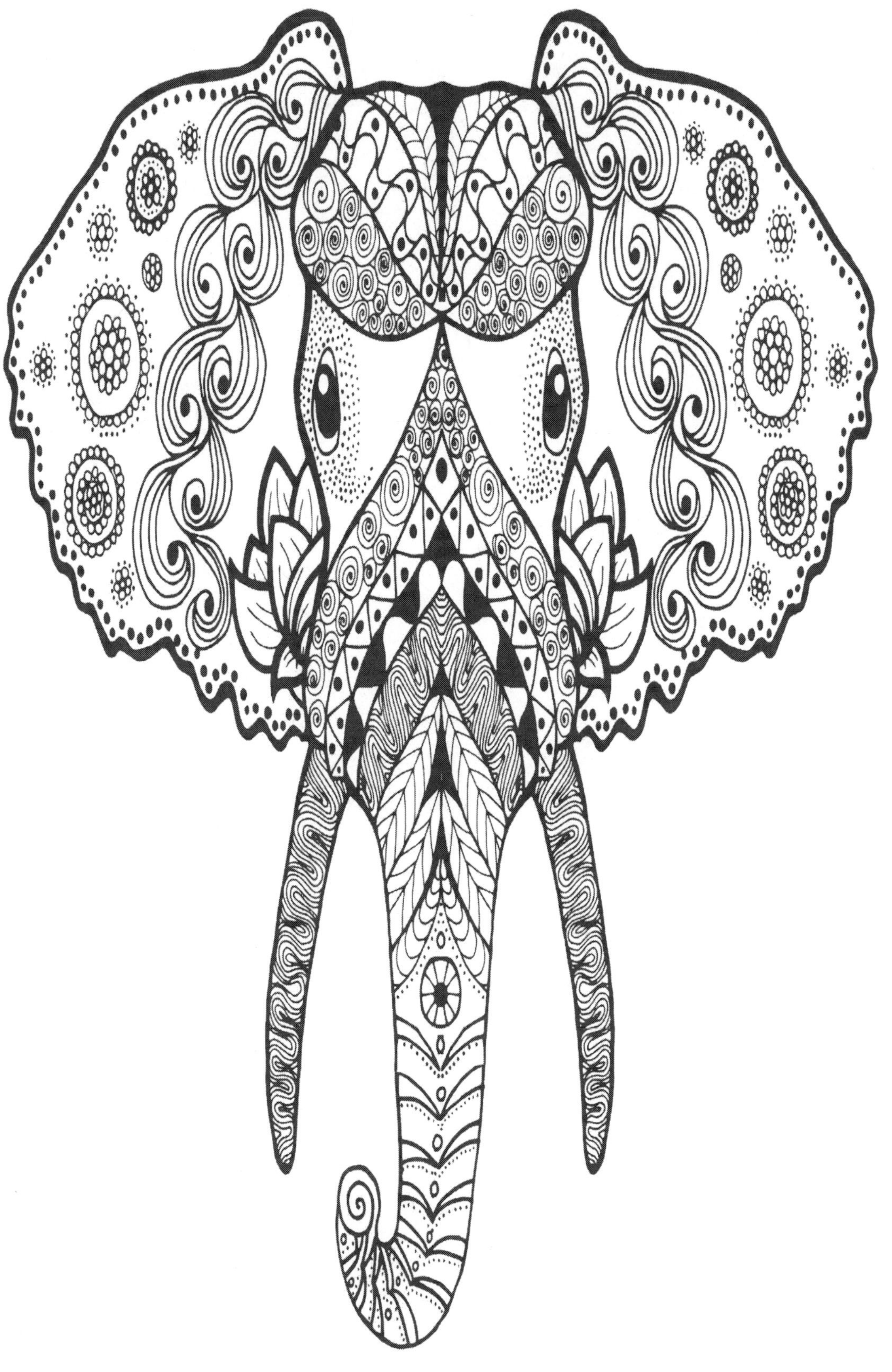

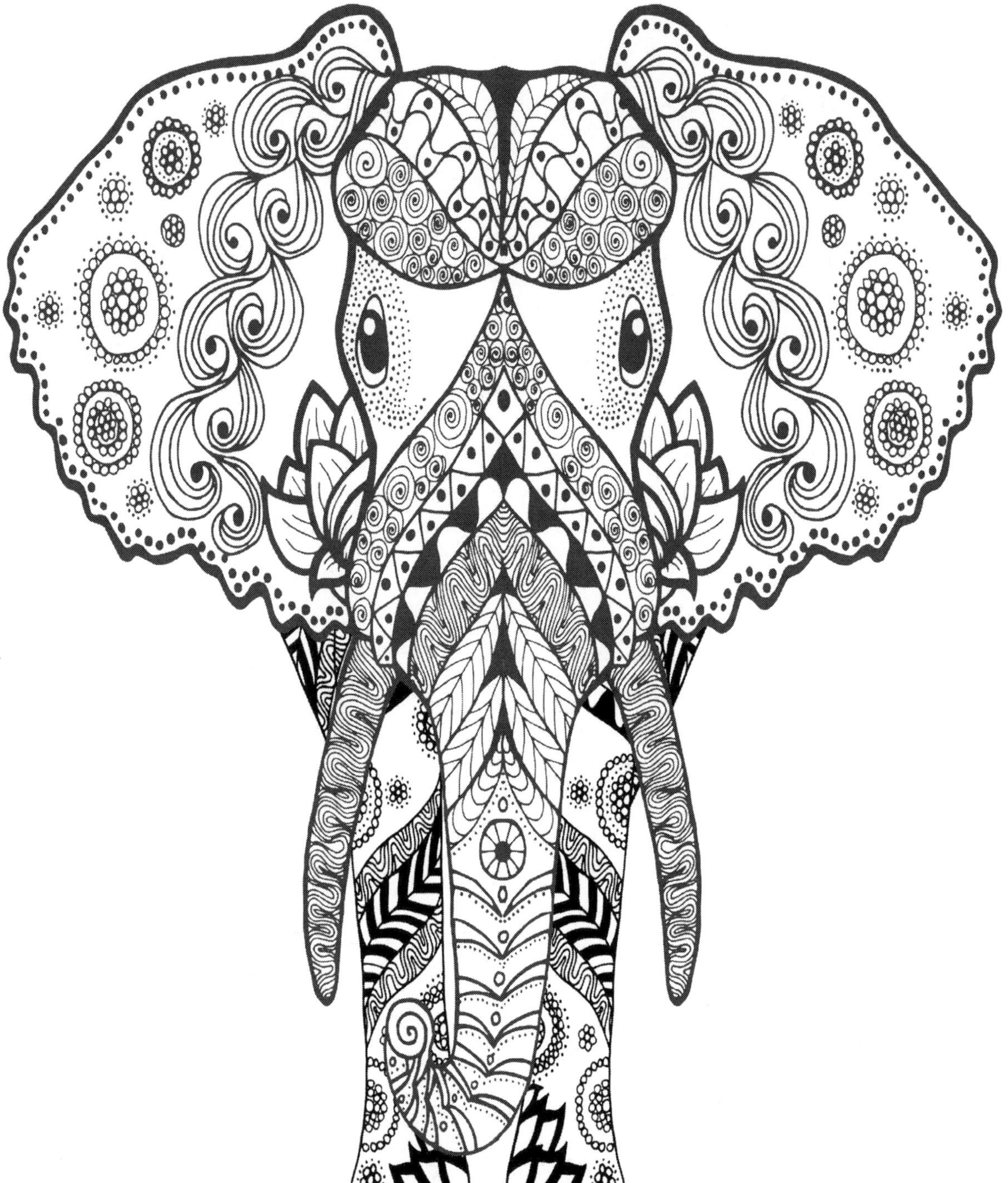

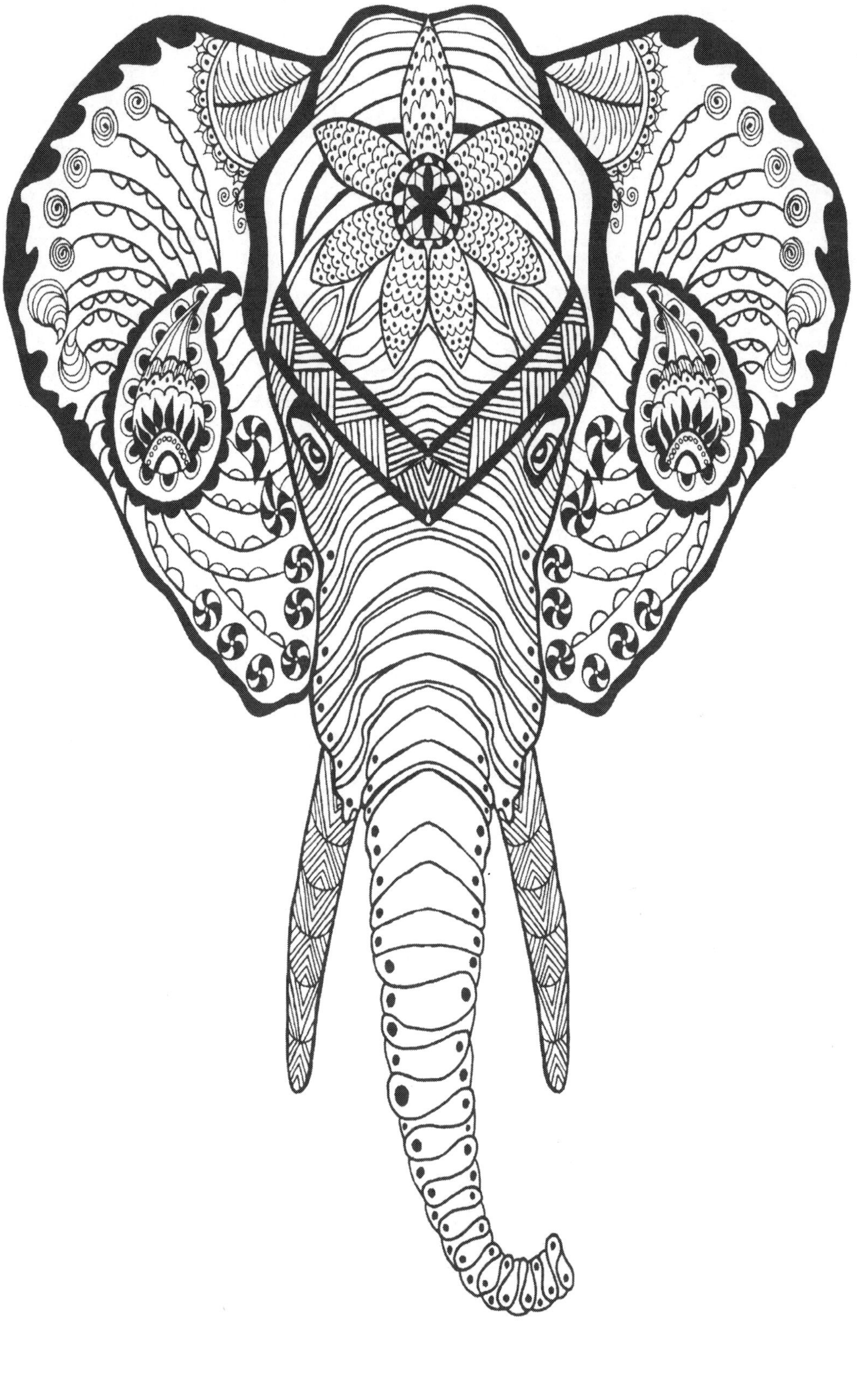

Made in the USA
Lexington, KY
27 December 2015